AF446535

Waves
The Hug of Nature

Waves: The Hug of Nature

Disclaimer

Please note that the scientific concepts presented in this book have been simplified to enhance comprehension for young readers. While accuracy is prioritized, certain details may have been adjusted or excluded for clarity and accessibility. For a more comprehensive understanding of the subject matter, additional resources or further study may be beneficial.

Nature's Warm Hug:
The Wave Parade

In nature's great embrace, we find,

A wave parade of every kind.

From ocean's roar to whispers light,

They hug the world with all their might.

First, meet the ocean's mighty waves,

Crashing, splashing, like bold knights brave.

Their hug is strong, their energy grand,

Guiding ships to distant land.

Next, the gentle ripples on a lake, Softly swaying, no need to quake. Their hug is tender, their touch so mild,

Bringing peace to every child.

Then come the sound waves in the air,
Carrying music, laughter, and prayer.
Their hug is joyful, their melodies
sweet,
Making the world feel complete.
And then, the light waves dance,
From sunbeams bright, they do
enhance.
Their hug is warm, their glow divine,
In their embrace, we always shine.
Nature's waves, in their embrace,
Bring joy and wonder to every place.
In their hug, we find our home,
With nature's love, we'll never roam.

Fun Fact

Did you know that waves can be big like ocean waves or tiny like the ones we use to talk on the phone? Waves come in all shapes and sizes!

Waves

Waves are like invisible wiggles or ripples that move through things like water, air, or even through the ground! They can make things sway or jiggle, and we can see them in the ocean waves, hear them in music, and even feel them when we play drums!

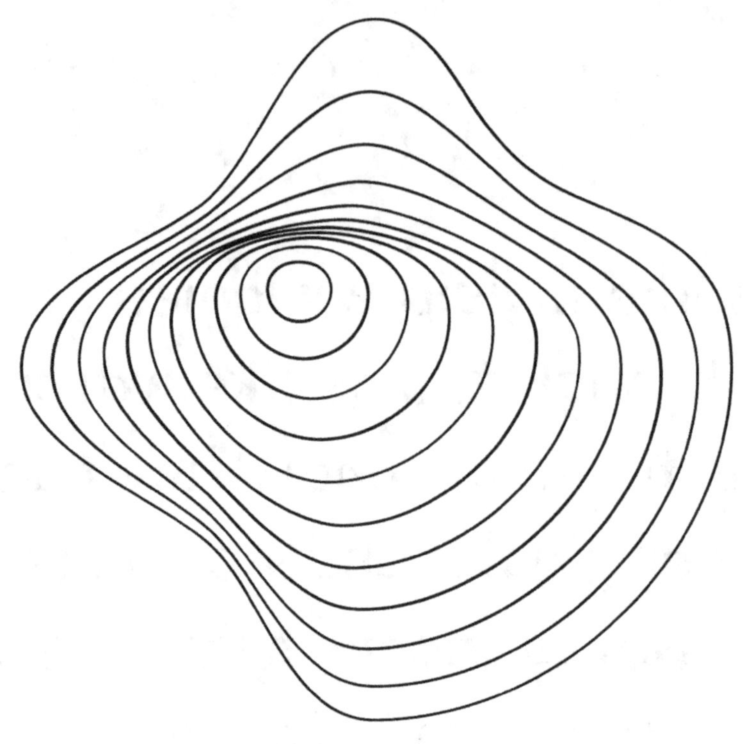

Fun Fact

Some waves are so small we can't even see them! But they're still there, helping us talk to friends on the other side of the world or see beautiful rainbows in the sky!

Waves Around Us

Embark on a thrilling adventure through the Maze of Waves! There are three paths to explore, each one leading to a different type of wave. Guide your object to its matching wave destination

Waves aren't just fun—they're home to playful dolphins and surfing fish! So next time you're at the beach, keep an eye out for those waves—they're nature's awesome playground!"

Water Waves

Those big waves you see at the beach? They're like nature's hug from the ocean! And surfing? It's like riding a roller coaster on a surfboard! The wind creates the waves, and surfers balance and do tricks.

Answer the following questions

1. Which scenario would create waves similar to those
   made in the water wave experiment?
   a. A person gently placing a leaf on the water's surface.
   b. A dog jumping into a swimming pool.
   c. A bird flying overhead.

2. What would happen if you tapped the water with the
   straw more forcefully in the experiment?
   a. The waves would become smaller.
   b. The waves would become bigger.
   c. The waves would stay the same size.

3. Which action would not create waves in the water?
   a. Blowing air across the water's surface.
   b. Dropping a spoon into a glass of water.
   c. Turning on a light switch

You've become a wave expert! Next time
you're near water, watch for real waves
and remember this fun experiment!

Splashing Waves: A Fun Water Experiment!

Let's explore waves with a hands-on experiment! All you need is a shallow dish of water and a straw or stick. Fill the dish with water and gently tap the surface with the straw or stick.

The taps create ripples, which are like mini waves!

Fun fact
Sound waves can travel through different things, like air, water, or even solid objects! That's why you can still hear your mom calling you from another room, even if she's behind a closed door!
These special waves are called
Mechanical Waves
So, the next time you clap your hands or play with your favorite toy, remember, you're making sound waves dance all around you! How cool is that?"

Sound Waves

Ever wonder why we hear music or voices? It's all thanks to sound waves. Picture sound waves as little dancers moving through the air. When someone speaks or drums beat, these dancers wiggle, and that's how we hear sound!

Fun fact

Did you know that animals like dogs and bats can hear sounds that are too high for humans to hear? Their ears are like super detectives, picking up on high-pitched sounds that are too fast for us to catch! It's like they have secret ears for super-fast slides!

Have you ever noticed how some sounds, like a bird chirping, are high, while others, like a big drum, are low? Well, that's because of something called pitch! It's like when you hear a fast whoosh down a slide, it's high-pitched, and when it's slow, it's low-pitched.

Determine the pitch of the sounds depicted in these images

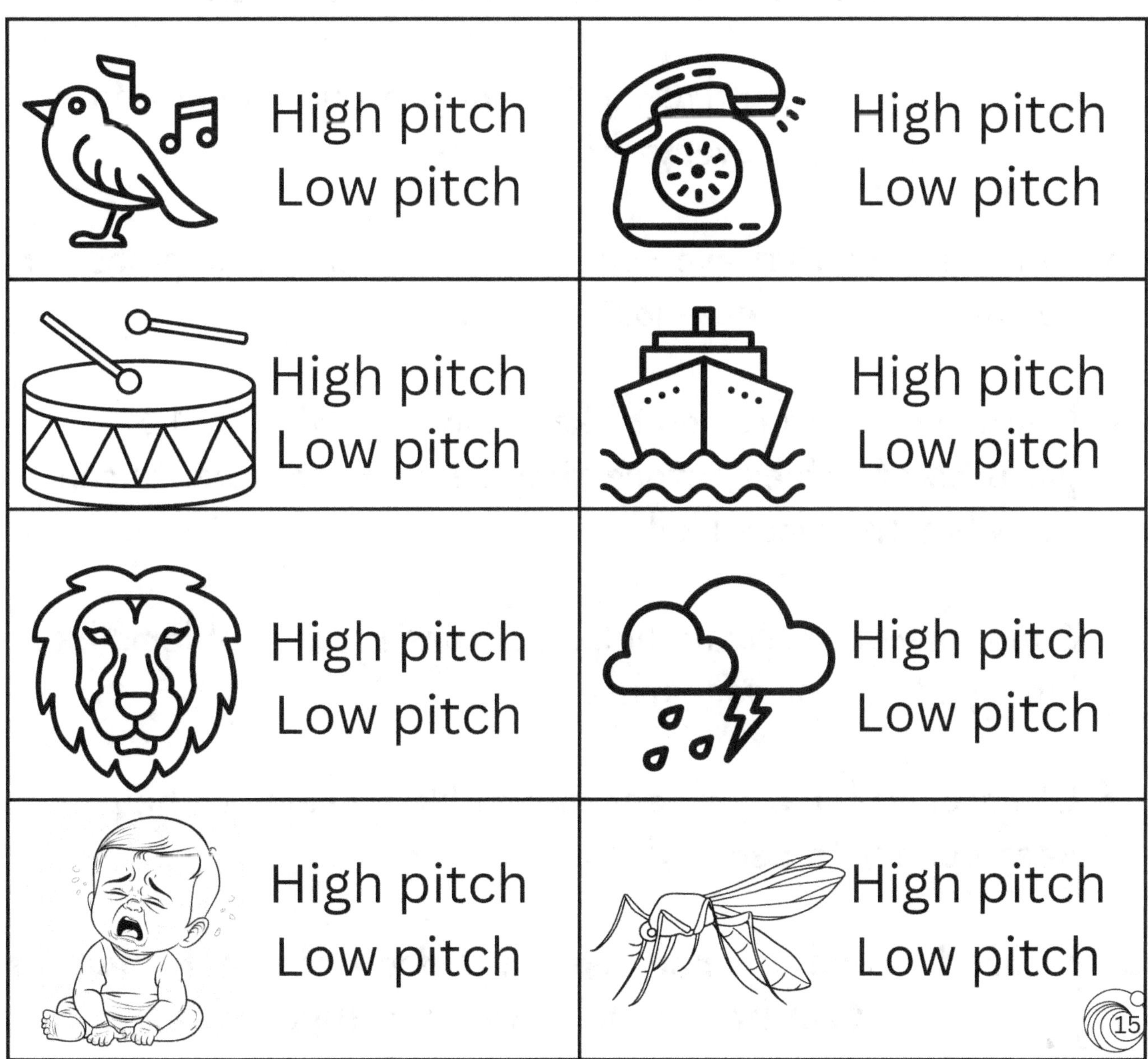

Here are some cool things to know about Ultrasound

- Ultrasound was invented a long time ago in the 1950s and it's super helpful for doctors all over the world.

- Ultrasound waves are like secret messages that go through our bodies, but they're too high-pitched for us to hear.

- Doctors use ultrasound to see inside our bodies without using radiation. It's safe for everyone, even babies!

- Doctors also use ultrasound to look at our organs and muscles to see if everything's okay.

- Did you know that even animals like dogs and dolphins can get ultrasound check-ups?

- Nowadays, doctors can make really cool 3D and 4D pictures of babies before they're born, so parents can see what they look like!

- Sometimes ultrasound helps doctors treat problems like kidney stones or sore muscles.

- Ultrasound can even clean things like jewelry or help keep our teeth healthy!

Ultrasound is like a super tool that doctors use to help us feel better and stay healthy!

Ultrasound

An ultrasound is like a magic camera that takes pictures inside your body using a special sound waves. It helps doctors see your organs and bones to make sure everything is okay. Did you know ultrasound can also help check on babies before they're born and even clean things like jewelry? It's pretty amazing! What else do you think ultrasound can do?

Caption each photo with a brief explanation of how Ultrasound is used in various situations.

Baby Waves

Exploring the Journey Before Birth

 **Heartbeat Monitoring** 

Thump, thump! Can you hear the babies' heartbeats? Doctors use waves to listen to their tiny hearts and make sure they're strong and healthy.

 **Movement Tracking** 

Wiggle, wiggle! The babies love to dance in mommy's tummy! Doctors use special waves to watch them move and make sure they're growing strong.

 **Gender Reveal** 

Boy or girl? Take a guess! Doctors use waves to show us if the babies are going to be brothers, sisters, or one of each!

 **Bonding with Babies** 

Hello, babies! Mommy and daddy are so excited to meet you! They look at your pictures and smile because they already love you so much.

Mommy's First Peek

Once upon a time, Daddy Beso and Mommy Judy went to visit the doctor for a special appointment. With a gentle touch, the doctor moved the wand of the Ultrasound magical machine over Mommy Judy's tummy, and two tiny figures appeared on the screen! The doctor smiled and played the sound of both babies' heartbeats. Tears of happiness filled Mommy Judy's eyes. Filled with love and excitement, Mommy Judy and Daddy Beso left the office, grateful for the unexpected blessing of twins

Electromagnetic waves come in different sizes, like small, medium, and big, and each size does different things.

Radio Waves

These are the big waves, like the ones that help send music to your radio!

Microwaves

These waves are like the ones in your microwave oven at home. They make your popcorn pop and heat up your leftovers!

Infrared Waves

These waves are like the warmth you feel from the sun or a cozy blanket. They help us see things at night with special goggles!

Visible Light

These waves are what we see with our eyes! They come in all the colors of the rainbow. They help us see the world around us, from the blue sky to the colorful flowers.

Ultraviolet (UV) Waves

These waves come from the sun and can give us a nice tan, but they can also give us sunburn if we stay out in the sun for too long!

X-Rays

These are super special waves that doctors use to take pictures of the inside of our bodies when we're not feeling well.

Gamma Rays

These are the smallest and strongest waves! They come from space and can even go through thick walls! Scientists use them to study stars and planets far away.

These waves are like invisible magic all around us, making our world exciting and full of wonders!

EM Waves

Have you ever wondered how we can see things like colors, or how we can talk on the phone without using wires? Well, it's all thanks to something amazing called electromagnetic waves! EM waves.

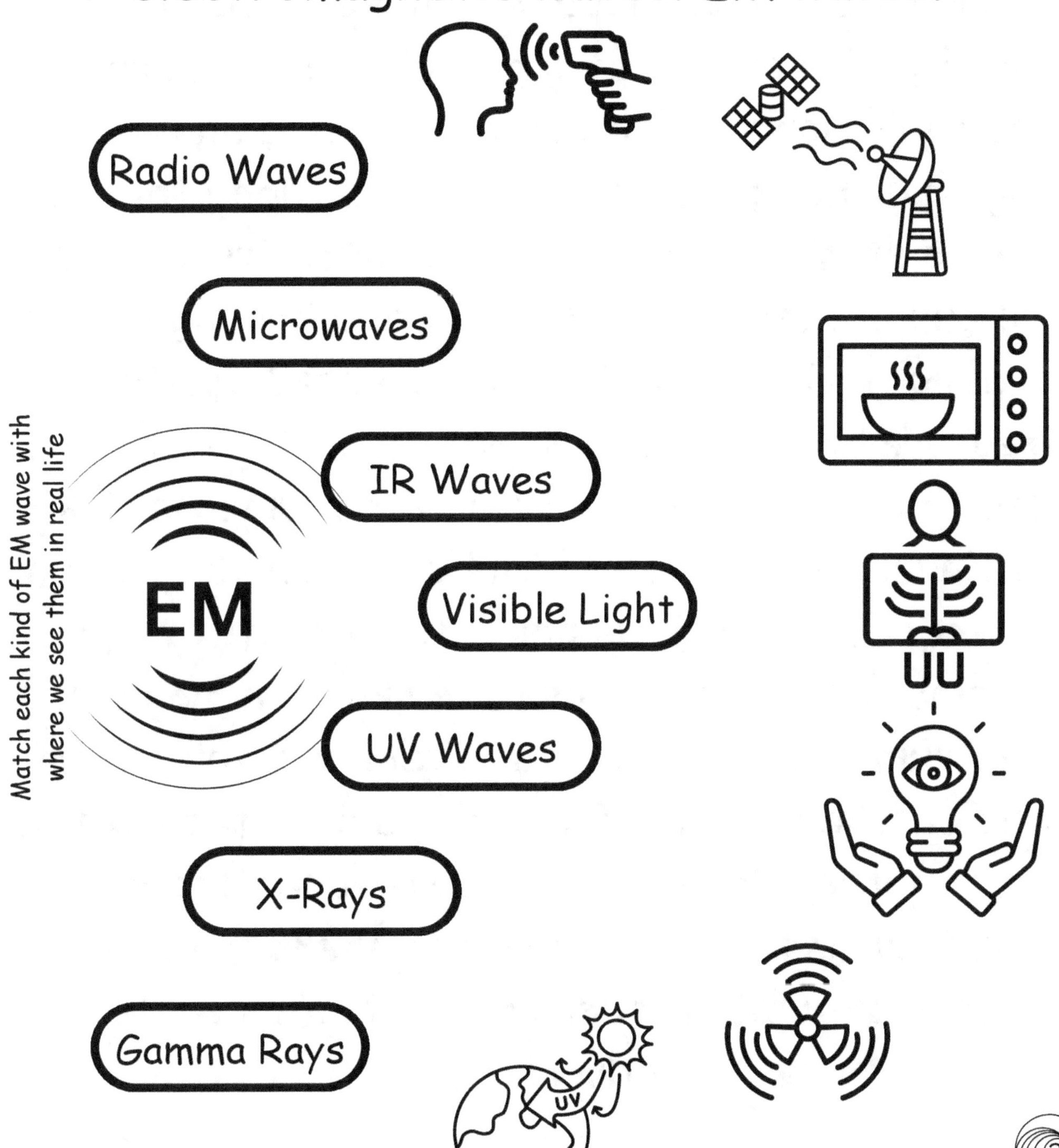

Seko's Spectacular EM Adventure

Once upon a time, in a world filled with wonders, there lived a curious boy named Seko. Seko went to a magical adventure unlike any other. The journey started with a burst of **light** that painted the sky with colors, leading Seko to a land where he could dance to the beat of the **radio** waves, singing along to his favorite tunes. Along the way, Seko stumbled upon a magical **microwave** that cooked his snacks in a blink, making him giggle with delight. Suddenly, Seko discovered a hidden treasure, a mysterious **X-ray** machine that could see through anything, like a secret spy! As Seko continued his quest, he reached a sparkling **prism**, where raindrops turned into a breathtaking rainbow, arching across the sky with magical **spectrum** of **color**s, each one telling its own story, and felt the rhythm of the world with the beat of its **frequency**. Finally, Seko discovered the source of all this magic - the boundless **energy** that filled his heart with wonder and fueled his endless adventure!

EM Waves

In this awesome word search puzzle, Seko needs your help to uncover the hidden words from his amazing EM adventure! Have fun!

EM Wordsearch Puzzle

M	G	T	J	F	U	B	W	G	E	A	M	S	N	Y
F	E	F	R	T	W	I	V	R	M	O	U	V	O	C
I	M	Y	J	H	L	B	M	P	W	T	D	G	R	N
T	E	N	S	G	Q	X	B	N	G	F	Z	I	B	E
D	X	W	S	I	B	W	X	R	P	V	O	O	T	U
R	F	D	N	L	M	I	C	R	O	W	A	V	E	Q
W	O	B	N	I	A	R	I	U	A	U	D	D	Y	E
J	U	V	C	X	M	S	A	O	R	Y	K	G	L	R
I	L	E	Y	D	M	U	K	W	Z	M	R	E	Y	F
X	Z	V	S	O	J	C	R	G	X	E	O	E	U	O
U	K	X	W	P	O	O	V	T	N	Q	M	U	I	C
H	P	U	N	K	J	L	U	E	C	W	A	D	J	K
T	P	H	L	O	Q	O	Z	W	W	E	A	B	Q	J
P	C	A	I	S	E	R	X	A	G	R	P	B	A	X
M	Y	C	B	W	R	P	U	O	R	C	Q	S	Y	R

Do you know how rainbows have all those pretty colors?

When sunlight goes through raindrops, it bends or changes direction.
But here's the cool part: different colors of light bend by different amounts. So, red bends a little, and violet bends a lot!
That's why when all the colors come out of the raindrops, they spread out into a rainbow shape with red on top and violet on the bottom. It's like nature's way of painting a beautiful picture in the sky!

What are the colors of the rainbow in order, starting from the top?

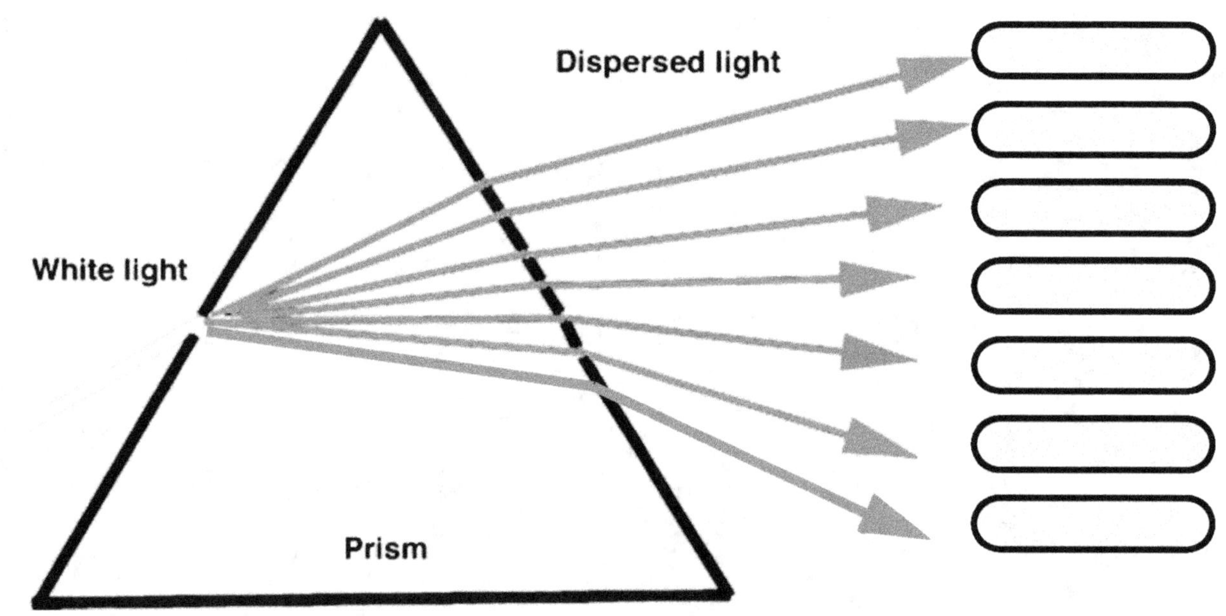

Light Waves

Light waves are like magical beams that help us see things around us, helping us see all the amazing things around us, from the blue sky to the colorful flowers in the garden!. They're part of the electromagnetic spectrum, which includes other invisible waves too.

Rainbow Magic: Prism Party!

When light goes through a prism, it splits into all the pretty colors like in a rainbow, showing us how light can bend and make colorful patterns!
Use a flashlight to shine light through a prism and see how it makes a rainbow!

The anatomy of waves is like knowing all the different parts that make up a wave, just like how we know all the parts of a toy or a puzzle!

Crest

The top part of a wave, like the peak of a hill or the highest point of a roller coaster.

Trough

The bottom part of a wave, like the dip between two hills or the lowest point of a roller coaster.

Amplitude

How tall a wave is from the middle to the top, like measuring how high a roller coaster goes.

Wavelength

How far apart two crests (or two troughs) of a wave are, like the distance between two hills.

Frequency

How often waves happen, like counting how many times a roller coaster goes up and down.

Wave Anatomy

Identify the different wave parts in each graph and then color the crests, the tippy-tops, in red, and the troughs, the low dips, in blue.

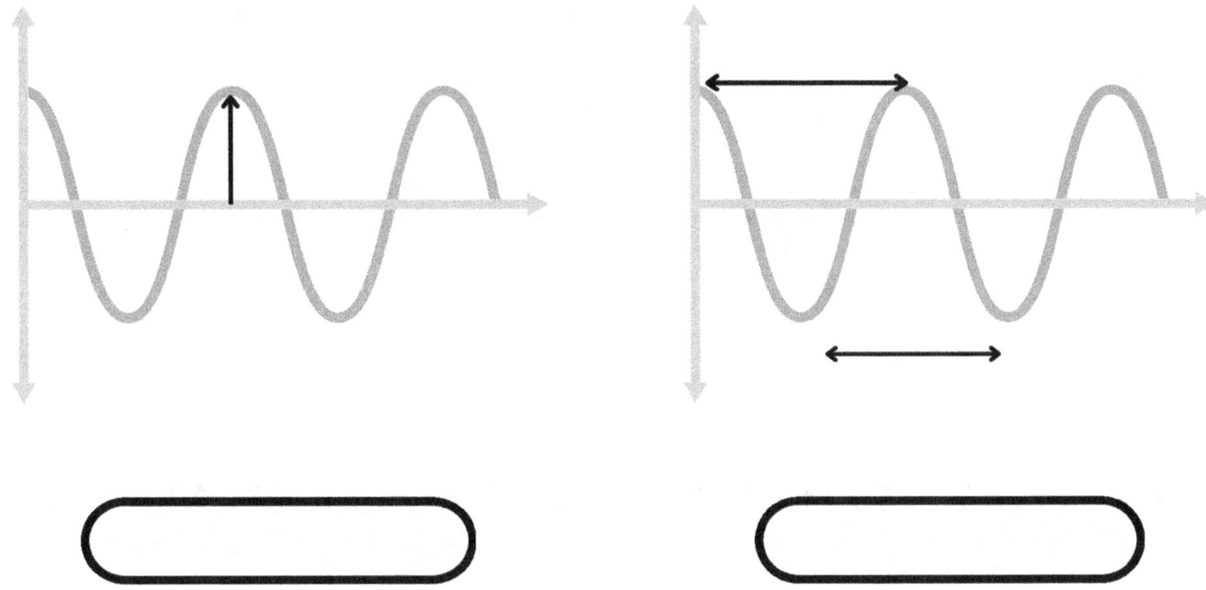

Follow the wave path and then decide which side is Low frequency and which is high frequency.

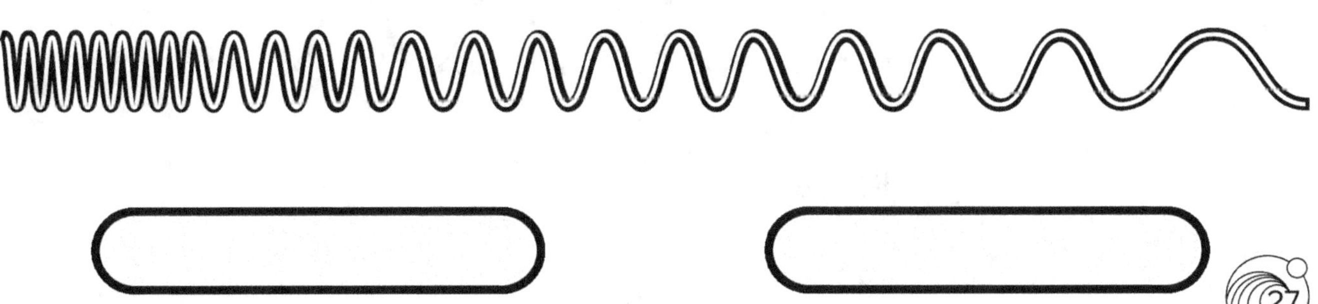

Categorize seismic waves as transverse, or as longitudinal.

Seismic waves are special waves that travel through the Earth
when there's an earthquake.
These waves shake things back and forth in the same direction
they're moving. It's like pushing and pulling something along
the ground.
Thus seismic waves are longitudinal.
Seismic waves help scientists understand how earthquakes
happen and how they affect the Earth.

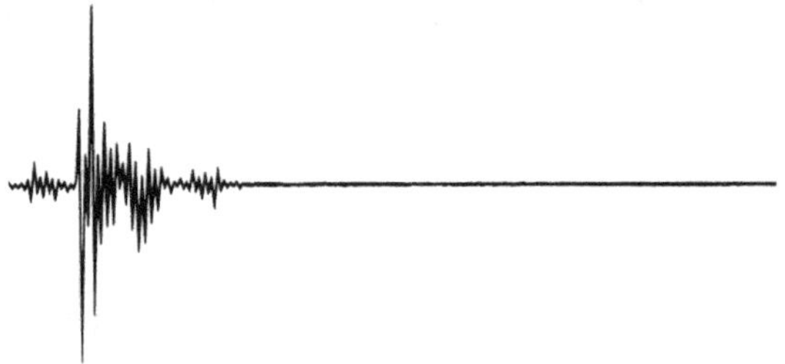

Categorize a water wave as transverse, or as longitudinal.

If you have ever been fishing and used a bobber you should
know the answer.
Firstly, the wave velocity is to the left.
Secondly, the bobber vibrates up and down.
Thus the water particles vibrate up and down.
Thus water waves are transverse waves.

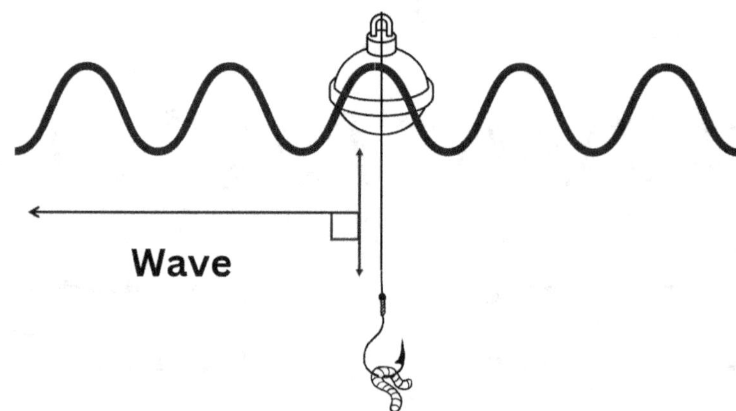

Types of Waves

There are two cool types: longitudinal and transverse. Longitudinal waves are like when you push and pull on a slinky toy, making it stretch and squish. Transverse waves are like when you shake a rope up and down

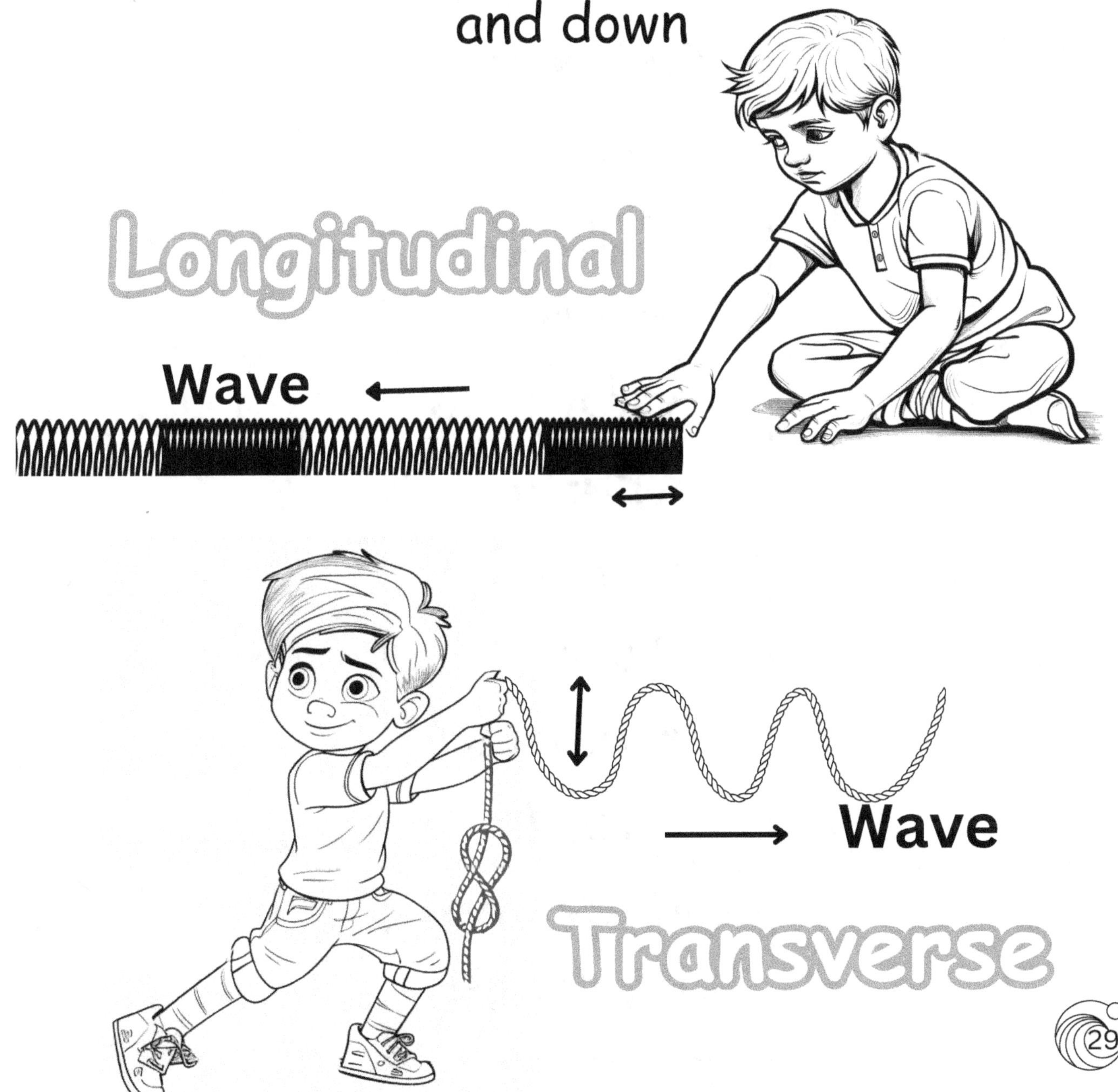

Time to crack this crossword puzzle! Here are the words you can use to fill it up and become a puzzle master

Amplitude Crest

Electromagnetic

Frequency

Longitudinal

Mechanical

Medium

Microwaves

Prizm

Rainbow

Seismic

Transverse

Trough

Ultrasound

Wavelength

Waves
The Hug of Nature

Across →

6. the number of waves that pass a point in a given time.
10. Created when sunlight goes through raindrops.
11. the material through which waves travel.
13. Waves that can travel through a vacuum, such as light waves.
14. Used to see inside our bodies without using radiation.
15. the highest point of a wave.

Down ↓

1. How tall a wave is from the middle to the top.
2. Waves like when you push and pull on a slinky toy.
3. Waves like when you shake a rope up and down.
4. Used to make popcorn and heat up leftovers!
5. How far apart two crests (or two troughs) of a wave are.
7. Waves that require a medium to travel through, such as air or water like sound waves.
8. the lowest point of a wave.
9. Waves that help scientists understand how earthquakes happen.
12. Splits light into all the pretty colors like in a rainbow.

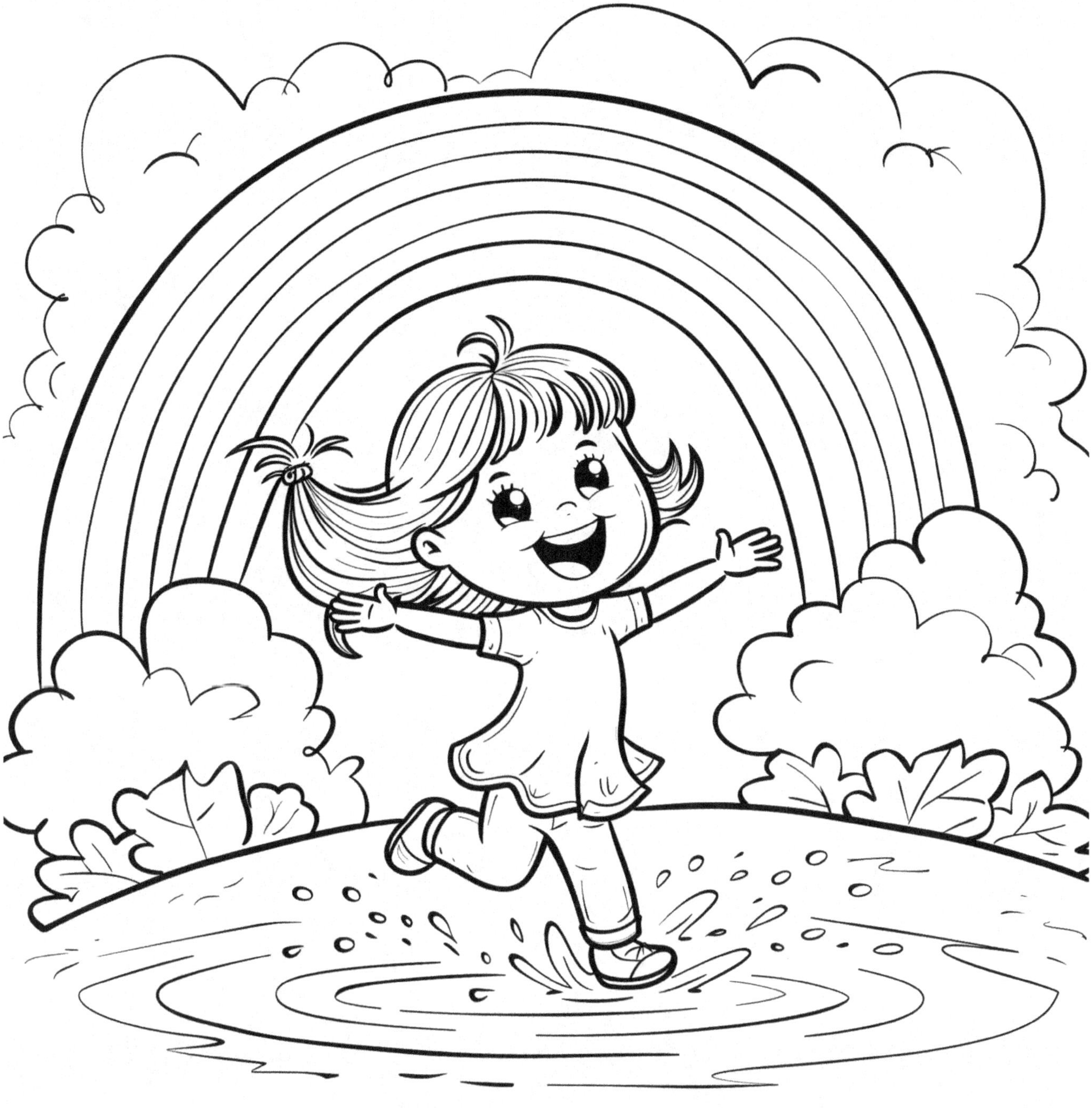

PHYSICS IS PHUN
PHYSICS IS JOYPHUL